Property Management Made Easy

For First-Time Rental Property Owners

Melissa DeLong

Copyright © 2014 Melissa DeLong

ISBN-10: 1482705885
ISBN-13: 978-1482705881

DEDICATION

This book is dedicated to all the landlords who went before us and were generous enough to share with us their wisdom so that we can now share it with you.

ACKNOWLEDGMENTS

Thanks to all the friends and family who helped make this book better through your generous contribution of time and energy: Melody, David, Dave, Margaret, Jim, Kelly, Todd, and Gid.

Contents

1. Introduction

If you are anything like we were when we started out, you are probably scared half out of your wits. You've just plunked down a huge chunk of money on a rental property based on profitability calculations in a spreadsheet. You've heard scary stories from other landlords and are now questioning your sanity. But turning theory into reality seems vaguely complicated. This book is designed to quell your fears and turn what looks hard into a simple process. Each chapter is designed to walk you, step by step, through the process of getting from the point where you've purchased your property to having a well-run rental management company.

Anyone who has spent time researching residential property management will have heard the horror stories. Our favorite is about a tenant who religiously paid his rent on time, until one day the checks just stopped coming. The landlord went to the house and discovered that the tenant had ripped up all the hardwood floors so that he could grow marijuana in the dirt between the floor joists. Apparently, after he took in the harvest it was time to find another location from which to do business. Stories like that are enough to make anyone think twice about investing in and managing residential properties.

The good news is that it is possible to manage rental properties without having major disasters happen. My husband and I started our business, Limerick Properties, in 2003. We've never been shorted a penny in rent and we've kept a 98% occupancy rate. This book is about sharing how we do it.

This book is for people who've already decided they want to invest in residential properties and are thinking about managing the properties themselves. There are lots of books out there that cover *why* property investment can be profitable, and this book is not about telling you *which* properties to purchase—we believe that you need local knowledge in order to make that investment decision well. Instead, this book is intended for the property manager who is getting into the market with his or her first property—or perhaps a handful of properties—and wants to know how the heck to manage them after they have been purchased, to avoid evictions, lost rent, liability, and property damage and thereby maintain long-term profitability and maximize his or her investment.

Managing your own properties may not be for you. There are companies out there that will manage the properties for you—show the property, collect the rent, evict tenants, and so forth. But you pay a big chunk of your potential profits to them, so we decided to manage them ourselves. Still, there may be circumstances in which paying a management company makes sense—if, for example, the property you are renting is located far from where you live. That might happen if you inherit your parents' house and decide to rent it for a while before selling it, or if you just don't have the time to dedicate to managing your own properties.

This book isn't comprehensive—it doesn't cover every possible situation that might occur. For example, it doesn't cover how to file your taxes, as that would make this book a thousand pages long and you would never read it. The brevity is intentional. We wanted to create a short and simple "how to" that will cover the most common situations and must-have advice for a new property manager. We wanted it to be a quick read so that you would indeed read every word. It's the what-we-wish-someone-had-told-us book. It is our hope that this book will help make you successful from the start, instead of having to learn too many things the hard way.

Disclaimer: The laws and regulations of each state, city, county, or local government vary, and this book is not intended to be a substitute for legal questions and advice. It is recommended you put together a business plan, using this book as a guide, and then review your plan with legal counsel to fully understand the obligations, responsibilities, and liabilities associated with becoming a landlord.

2. Setting Up Your Company

Before you purchase your first property, or at least before you start renting, we recommend that you get your company structure in place. It's important to do this for reasons of liability protection and to establish a professional company appearance for your rental applicants, tenants, and contractors.

If you operate your business as a corporation rather than as an individual, you gain some liability protection from being sued personally. For example, if your renter breaks a leg on the front steps, she can't sue you personally, she can only sue your company. The advantage to you is that this protects your personal savings and other assets from being awarded to someone in a lawsuit.

Often scammers will target private-party rentals because they figure you won't know how to protect yourself with background and credit checks, proper lease paperwork, and so forth. In other words, doing business as a private party paints a target on you. Doing business as a company, on the other hand, will scare a fair percentage of these scammers away.

The good news is that in most states it's pretty easy to get set up. This chapter details the basic steps.

Setting Up Your Company

Step 1	Company Name and Web Address
Step 2	Mailing Address
Step 3	Company Formation
Step 4	Business License
Step 5	Employer Identification Number
Step 6	Bank Account
Step 7	Taxes & Bookkeeping
Step 8	Property Title

Pick Your Company Name and Website Address

In choosing your company name, you want to make sure that it's unique. Do Internet searches on possible names. If the search finds a similarly named company that could be confused with yours, pick another name. You don't want to be easily confused with someone else, even if they do something completely different from property management. The worst thing would be if someone else with a similar name ranks at the top of the Google search engine so that your name doesn't make it onto the first page of search results.

The most important marketing tool you will have is your website, so whatever name you choose, you will want to secure the website address before you move forward with the paperwork to form your company. Purchase of the website address is cheap, so it makes sense to do it first. You don't want to go to all the work and expense of forming your company only to find that you can't purchase the Web address because someone else is already using it. Your name shouldn't be easy to misspell either, because that will make it more difficult to find your website.

The Web address, also called a domain name, is the address a customer will use to find your website. Ours is **www.limerickproperties.com**. You will want yours to be **www.mycompanyname.com**. Don't use other extensions, such as .net or .org, because .com is the most common for commercial business purposes and that is what people will naturally try first. You want your website address to be easy to find and remember, so making it the same as your company name makes sense.

There are lots of companies out there selling domain names. However, it's important to use a reputable company that purchases the domain on your behalf. Some companies will buy the domain for themselves because they know you want it, and then they will rent you the use of it. The difference is that if you own the domain name you can keep it forever (as long as you pay the small yearly renewal fee) and you can move the domain name to any registrar of your choice. Less-reputable companies will rent you the domain name, perhaps raising the prices unreasonably every year, and will not let you transfer the name to another registrar. These companies can effectively hold your website address hostage because they own it.

Examples of reputable domain registration companies are **www.dotster.com** and **www.godaddy.com**. If you go to these websites you will immediately see a search box in the middle of the page, where you can look to see whether the Web address you want for your company is available. Go ahead and purchase the Web address at this point, before investing further in setting up your company, to ensure someone else doesn't purchase it in the meantime. You may also want to purchase similar website names so that you can redirect misspellings to your main site. So, for example, if your website name will be **www.mycompanYname.com**, you might also purchase **www.mycompanIESname.com**.

Get a Mailing Address

Now that you are going to be a big bad landlord, you really don't want renters to know where you live. In the event that you do end up in a dispute or an eviction, you don't want an angry tenant showing up at your house. So you need an alternate address from which to do business, where people can send their rent checks.

You can get a post office box at the post office. However, this screams "this isn't our real address." Another option is to get a box at a private mailbox vendor such as a UPS store or Pony Express. The advantage is that this address will look like a physical office location. Ours is 11410 NE 124th Street, Suite 317, Kirkland, WA. Another advantage to using a private mailbox rather than a PO Box is that they will accept mail from any vendor, such as UPS or FedEx, whereas people can't send an overnight FedEx package to a PO Box.

Pick a convenient mailbox location, where you can pick up your mail at least once a week. You will want to secure this mailing address before starting all the paperwork on your company formation, so that you can start using this address from the very beginning and avoid using your home address.

Company Formation

You will want to form a company and operate all the business of the rentals from within the company structure, to help protect you in terms of liability. As we mentioned, if someone trips and breaks her leg on the front porch, operating the business within a legal corporate structure means that person won't be successful at suing you personally. She can't take away your personal assets; she can only sue the company. So this is a critical step in getting set up to operate your business in a way that protects your personal savings or assets.

You will represent everything you do, both with renters and with people you pay to do work on the property, as being with your company. You are no longer George, the guy who has some rentals down the street, and instead have just become George, president of Charming Properties LLC. Tenants will write their checks to your company, not to you personally. You will sign all correspondence and e-mails with your title and your company name. You *never* want someone to claim they were confused about who they were doing business with. If anyone can claim that they did business with you personally instead of with your company, they can then sue you personally and the liability protection of having a company will be null and void.

There are a number of different kinds of companies—C corporations, S corporations, or limited liability companies (LLCs). Each structure has pros and cons, which we won't try to explain in detail here. It's best to consult an attorney if you are not familiar with which type you want and why. And rules governing corporate structures vary from state to state, because it is state law that governs corporate set up and use. However, if you are planning to remain small and will not have partners in your business, and if you want to minimize tax paperwork, an LLC is the likely choice. If you are a sole proprietor (that is, if you don't have any partners—except your spouse, in a community property state), using an LLC structure enables you to file your personal federal taxes without a separate corporate filing. So an LLC can hugely simplify the work of maintaining a company structure.

There are a number of online websites that can help you to get set up. These do-it-yourself sites are a very viable alternative to paying an attorney, if you are comfortable doing the work yourself. Reputable sites such as **www.rocketlawyer.com** or **www.nolo.com** will walk you through the process and charge minimal fees in comparison to using a private attorney. The process typically consists of two parts. First, you draft your corporate structure documents, which say what your company does, how you will be structured (the number of corporate officers and so forth), and who owns the company. Second, you will file these documents with the secretary of state in the state where you plan to incorporate.

Getting Your Business License

Your local government—at the state, county, or city level—may require you to have a business license to operate in its municipality. Washington State, where we live, requires a state business license, which we received when we filed for our LLC. However, every local government is different. Discovering the local business licensing requirements in your area will require some research on your part.

Getting an Employer Identification Number

Even if you won't have any employees, you still need an employer identification number from the Internal Revenue Service. An EIN is like a social security number for your company. Due to U.S. banking regulations, you won't be able to open a bank account in your company name without one. Just go to **www.irs.gov** and search for "Apply for EIN" to find where you can complete the online form. You will get your EIN assigned right on the website.

One of the things that completing the EIN paperwork does is to tell the IRS how you will file your taxes. There are two choices: either you will file a separate tax return for your company (which is more work for you or your accountant) or you can elect to include your rental company on your personal 1040, as if you were doing business personally (which is less work). In order to avoid filing a separate corporate tax return, you need to be an LLC—not a C or an S corporation—and you must be classified as a sole proprietorship. This means your LLC can't have any members (analogous to a stockholder in a C or an S corporation) other than yourself—and your spouse, if you live in a community property state. Electing not to file a separate tax return will not affect the liability protection you get from having an LLC, but it simplifies your tax filing.

Opening a Bank Account

One of the most critical things you will need to do to maintain your company structure is to keep your personal finances separate from your company's finances. Failure to keep them separated can invalidate the liability protections provided by the corporate structure. For example, if someone can prove that money you took from them was deposited into your personal bank account, they may be able to sue you personally—making it possible for them to go after your personal savings or assets. So you must keep your personal finances separate from your company at all times. If your company needs funds to pay property expenses and there isn't enough funds in the company checkbook, transfer the money into the corporate account from your personal account and then pay the expenses out of the business account. The funds transferred into the company will be considered an investment by the stockholders, whereas if you pay the expenses directly from your personal account, this will invalidate the corporate structure.

Hence, opening a bank account is critical to keeping your corporate structure intact. It may be convenient to have your corporate bank account at the same bank where you do business personally, which simplifies the transfer of funds between accounts when needed. You also may want to consider the bank's Web banking capabilities, if you want to be able to take care of the bulk of your banking needs without having to visit the bank in person.

The bank will require copies of your EIN paperwork as well as your corporate structure documents in order to open the bank account; this is why you must do those steps first.

Taxes and Bookkeeping

Whether you choose to tackle your taxes and bookkeeping yourself or hire an expert depends on your level of tolerance for reading fine print and thrashing your way through arbitrary and capricious tax forms. If business accounting is not something you are familiar with, be sure to get a good bookkeeper when you start your business, and before you start renting. Your bookkeeper can tell you what record keeping you need to do from the start to make the eventual tax filing and bookkeeping process easier.

Property Title

When we purchase a property, we typically purchase it in our names, personally, because this allows us to get the best loan rates on the mortgage. But this presents a problem because it breaks the rule about keeping the business and personal finances separate to protect the validity of our LLC. To mitigate this risk, we quitclaim deed the properties into the name of the LLC after the purchase goes through escrow. This is a very simple filing with the county in which the property is located, to change the name on the title. We can do this in Washington State because our state tax laws allow a change of title in name only. Because we own both the LLC and the property, the State of Washington sees the change of name on the title as being irrelevant for tax purposes—so we don't incur any sales or excise tax. You should check with your escrow agent about the viability of this in your state.

There is however a theoretical risk in retitling the property into the name of the LLC, which is that the bank could decide that the property is no longer securing their loan and could call the loan as due immediately. However, the loan in question should have been set up with the bank with the understanding that it is not a primary residence, meaning that the lender agreed to the loan with full knowledge that the property was an investment and would be used as a rental. And if we got into a dispute with the bank, it's simple enough to retitle the property back into our personal names.

You should check with your attorney and escrow agent when you purchase your property, and decide whether you want to retitle the property in the name of your company based on your local state and county laws.

3. Setting Up Your Rental Systems

Once you have your corporate structure complete, you will need to get a few things in place before you start advertising your property for rent, so that you are ready to process rental applications.

Setting Up Your Rental Systems

Step 1	Renter Screening Account
Step 2	Application & Walk-Through Checklist
Step 3	Fax Number
Step 4	Key Organization
Step 5	Tenant Move-In Information
Step 6	Backup Contact
Step 7	Property Maintenance

Open a Renter Screening Account

You will *never* rent a property without running a credit check first, so you will need to set up an account with a credit check agency. We use **www.amerusa.net**, which has always worked well for us, but there are a number of online companies out there to choose from.

Keep in mind that when you get applications they will contain confidential personal information such as social security numbers. It's important to keep this information secure. If you are going to keep the information on your computer, be sure to have a password on your computer so that people coming and going from your house cannot access it. If you are going to keep the information in paper format, it needs to be in a locked file cabinet. Treat applicants' information the way you would want your information to be treated.

There are two different types of credit checks you can run. The basic level allows you to submit a request to the credit reporting agency and get summary credit information. Account numbers and other confidential information are omitted from this report. Typically, these reports can only be faxed or e-mailed to you during the credit reporting agency's business hours, because you have to request that they run the report for you.

The more advanced level of access allows you to run the credit check online 24/7 and get the full results immediately. This is a huge advantage if you are doing part-time property management and will often receive and process applications in the evenings or on weekends. However, this higher level of access to credit information requires that the credit agency verify that you know how to properly protect confidential information. This requires an on-site inspection—which primarily means they want to see that you have that locking file cabinet in which to secure information.

The level of access you choose depends on whether you want to be able to run credit checks at any time of day and whether you want the full credit report or just the summary information. We operated on the basic level for the first few years and it worked fine, until we decided it would be easier to be able to process the credit checks in the evenings when we were at home.

Get a Lease Application and Walk-Through Checklist

In order to get the information you need to evaluate a potential tenant, you will need the renter to sign a lease application. This application will collect information such as the renter's social security number so you can run his or her credit history, prior landlord contact information, employment and income information, and so on. It will also include a legal release that authorizes you to access their credit report and employment information.

Before you turn over the keys to your tenant, you also will want to do a walk-through to inspect for any damages. There is more information about this in chapter 11, "When Your Renter Moves In."

Both the walk-through checklist and the lease application forms can be purchased through a legal forms website such as **www.rocketlawyer.com** or **www.nolo.com**.

Get a Fax Number
You will want a fax number where renters can send you their rental application form. We have a fax number but no fax machine, so we don't pay monthly charges for a dedicated fax line. There are services that will give you a phone number for a small fee, and then when someone sends a fax to your phone number the service converts the fax to a PDF and e-mails it to you. There are a ton of these companies out there, such as **www.faxbetter.com**.

Organize Your Keys
We had three rental houses before we lost track of which key belonged to which lock at which house. It gets worse when you start to change the locks each time a tenant moves out. Develop a system to keep track or, trust us here, you'll regret it. You'll have a giant ring of keys and you'll have to try every one of them to find the right key to any lock.

Tenant Move-In Information
When a tenant moves in they will need to know things like who the electric company is so they can set up service in their name. You will want to have a form for each property, which you give your tenant that includes the contact information for the electric, gas, water, sewer, garbage, telephone, and cable TV companies. You may also wish to provide tenants with other helpful but optional resources such as the contact information for your house cleaner, carpet cleaner, or insurance agent.

Having a Backup Contact
Remember that, as much as you plan to do yourself, you won't always be available. You do want to go on vacation someday, right? So you will need to develop a backup to cover for you when you aren't available. This can be a family member you trust and who is handy with household maintenance problems, or maybe a handyman with whom you've developed strong trust over the years. But in any case, be sure that you have someone available and that your tenants have their contact information in case you aren't available.

Property Maintenance
Unlike your personal household, you won't see your rental properties every day. That means you won't see when the gutters are overflowing, sending water onto the house siding, or when the kitchen sink needs to be recaulked before water damage occurs in the cabinet below. So you need to become

more systematic about inspecting for damage and maintenance issues. You will probably have some tenants who have owned houses, and you will learn over time that you can count on them to alert you to any possible issues. But generally you will want to find excuses to visit occasionally so you can take a look around and see whether anything needs attention.

However, the law in most states requires that you give your tenant notice of any inspection on the property. Don't think that because you own it means you can enter the property anytime you want. Once it's rented, your tenant has the right to privacy. Check your local laws to ensure you know what kind of notice is required and how far in advance you need to let a tenant know you will be visiting. There are legal exceptions for emergencies, so if there is water leaking, for example, you don't have to wait two days to enter the property and fix it. This also doesn't apply if the tenant requests you to come and address an issue.

You will be replacing carpet and washing machines, and unplugging sewer lines, more often than you ever imagined. Even if you are handy and plan to do a lot of the maintenance yourself, you will need a network of resources to help out. Because, trust us, a water heater will die when you are on vacation, not on a Saturday afternoon when you had nothing better to do. Develop a resource list before it's 3 a.m. and your tenant calls in desperation because his kitchen is flooded due to a broken pipe. Your real estate agent is a great source for recommendations. The minimum list of resources you should have handy from the start includes plumber, electrician, roofer, furnace repair, pest/bug control, and septic cleaner/repair. Other resources you will want to develop over time include a carpet cleaner, house cleaner, landscaper, and painter.

There are a number of maintenance items you need to address before a tenant moves in, and a great time to inspect the property is when you are between tenants. Develop your own checklist based on the needs of your particular properties. Here are a few of the common things you will want to do:

- ✓ Change the batteries in smoke detectors and carbon monoxide detectors
- ✓ Change the locks
- ✓ Clean carpets
- ✓ Have the property cleaned, as needed
- ✓ Inspect landscaping
- ✓ Inspect attic and crawl spaces for issues such as pests, water damage, and mold
- ✓ Have septic system pumped and serviced (every few years)
- ✓ Inspect sinks, tubs, and showers for damaged caulk
- ✓ Change furnace filters
- ✓ Clean and inspect dryer vents
- ✓ Replace any burned-out lightbulbs

4. Getting Property Insurance

For the most part, insurance for your rental property is very similar to the insurance you get on your personal home, except that it covers you as a landlord. You will get a policy that insures the property against the usual perils such as fire, floods, and earthquakes. If you are relying on a loan to make your rental purchase, your lender will require that your policy be in place at the time of closing. If you are paying cash for the property, don't forget this critical step, even if there is no bank forcing the issue.

Even if you already own rental properties, it is a good idea to review your coverage with an insurance agent experienced in landlord policies, who can help guide you through getting the most effective and cost-effective coverage.

Your Landlord Policy

There are a few things that will be different from your own homeowner policy, which you will want to think about and ask your agent about:

- **Liability coverage.** Pay close attention to the liability coverage, which will help to protect the assets within the corporation should your renter sue you for any reason.

- **Personal property coverage.** The coverage for personal property (the stuff inside the house) will typically be lower than the coverage on your personal house, because you don't have furniture and clothes at the property. However, the personal property coverage still must cover the contents of the property, such as the appliances, which are not considered part of the structure itself.

- **Type of policy.** Insurance policies come in two flavors: inclusive and excluded. An inclusive policy states the specific perils it *will* cover (i.e., what's included). An excluded policy states the specific perils it *will not* cover (i.e., what's excluded). The better policies are excluded policies that explicitly state what they will not cover. For example, a policy that says it will cover everything except earthquakes would cover your property if it were to burn down, if it were to get hit by a meteor from outer space, or any other weird thing that might happen. You can decide whether you are OK with the policy not covering earthquakes and choose whether to pay for additional earthquake coverage. Contrast this to a policy that says it will cover only fire and floods. That policy doesn't cover anywhere near all the things that might possibly happen to the property. So make sure your policy is one that says specifically what *isn't* covered, and then decide if you are content with that list.

Renters Insurance

We require all of our tenants to obtain a renters insurance policy, and we strongly recommend that you do the same. This policy does not insure the structure, but does insure the tenant's property that is located at the property. For example, this would cover the tenant's couch if a pipe bursts, floods the house, and damages furniture.

You should require the tenant to name your company as an additional insured on the renters policy. This doesn't cost the tenant anything additional. However, it will go a long way toward quelling disputes between insurance companies. If that pipe bursts and damages the tenant's furniture, the tenant's insurance company won't try to collect from you as being liable for the pipe bursting, because you are named as an insured on their policy. Your own insurance policy will cover the damage the burst pipe caused to the house itself. If your tenant had some responsibility for the burst pipe— say, if he left the heat off in the house during a cold snap and the pipe froze—the renters insurance may help pay for the damage to the house. However, you as the landlord would leave the two insurance companies to work that out between them.

This came in super handy once for us when a tree from a neighbor's yard fell on our tenant's truck. Figuring out who was liable was painful because our tenant claimed that we knew the neighbor's trees were in bad shape. It's not clear how we would have known this, but logic doesn't always prevail when people are angry. Because we were named as an additional insured on the renters policy, however, the insurance company paid without ever coming back against us.

5. Deciding On Your Rental Policies

This chapter covers some of the issues you will want to consider in advance of advertising, so you will have the answers handy when the phone starts to ring. Before deciding on your policies, however, you must first get familiar with your local landlord laws. Different states, counties, and cities will have their own regulations. Do your homework. The fastest way to get in trouble in court is to have a clause ruled illegal because it contradicts local laws.

In Washington State, a residential lease cannot extend for longer than twelve months. We've had tenants ask for longer-term leases, and although that sounds good, such a lease would be invalidated in court—even though it was the tenant requesting the longer term. You need to have a grasp of the basics of your local tenant–landlord laws to stay out of trouble.

Although we've documented here the policies we have set, you may decide on different policies based on what works for your properties. You can even have different policies for different properties. For example, while we normally do not allow smoking, we might consider allowing it at a property where the owner we bought it from smoked and the property has already been permeated with smoke smell.

Landscaping
Who will care for the landscaping? If you expect the tenants to keep the yard up, consider a rebate for this. Send the tenants a quarterly check for a minimal amount after you've seen that they have kept up the yard for the previous three months. If they don't keep the yard up, then use the funds to pay a landscaper to clean up. This is much better than a scheme of offering lower rent in exchange for yard maintenance, which offers you little recourse if the tenants don't hold up their end of the deal.

Credit Score

We cover the topic of credit scores in more detail in chapter 10, "Choosing a Tenant". You may want to publish your minimum credit score requirement as part of your corporate policies, because this helps to reduce the number of applications from people with credit ratings below your minimum.

Pets

We sometimes allow dogs, if they have good pet references—a prior landlord who can verify no dog issues or damage. We don't allow any dangerous breeds such as pit bulls, regardless of an owner's assurances that they are "the sweetest little thing." There will be another renter along in a minute without a potentially aggressive dog. The property's neighbors will thank you, and you will minimize your own liability.

We don't allow cats under any circumstances. This might seem odd, given that we do allow dogs. But the reality is that some cats spray and ruin not only carpets but also the plywood flooring underneath. To get rid of the cat smell you may have to replace both the carpets and the underlying plywood. We choose not to take that chance. Most dog owners have trained their dogs not to use the carpet as their bathroom, but in our experience cats don't always stick to the litter box.

You might choose differently than we have on dogs and cats. Just think about it and be firm in your decision on pets, because people will beg you to change your policy. Some landlords will collect additional security deposits when people have pets.

Smoking

Our properties are all nonsmoking. This isn't because we are trying to encourage people to quit; it's because we don't want our properties permanently impregnated with the smoke smell.

Security Deposits

Our security deposit is roughly equivalent to one month's rent. Upon lease signing, we collect the first month's rent and the security deposit. This is a bit different from most landlords, who collect a security deposit of a few hundred dollars plus first and last months' rent. The cash required to get into our property is the same as to get into other properties, so it doesn't matter to the tenant. However, we prefer a higher security deposit because it's more protection for us should something get damaged, and in our state we can deduct unpaid rent from the security deposit upon lease termination anyway.

Application Fee

We charge a nonrefundable application fee for each adult who will live at the property. This mostly just covers the cost of the credit check and is intended to filter out anyone who isn't serious.

Late Fee

We charge a late fee for each day that adds up fast to a maximum of 10% of one month's rent. This is a stiff late fee, so most of the time it is an effective deterrent to late payments. We've seen other landlord policies that state that if a tenant is more than five days late with payment twice during the lease term two things happen: first, the lease immediately changes to a month-to-month lease, which makes it easier to later terminate and evict; and second, the rent increases by $100 per month. While these are pretty onerous clauses, they do help to deter people from paying late.

6. Designing Your Lease Document

Because landlord laws vary from state to state, you will need a lease document that adheres to the laws in your area. There are numerous websites from which you can purchase a standard lease contract that you can use over and over. Both **www.rocketlawyer.com** and **www.nolo.com** can supply you with a contract for your state. Be sure to add to your lease any of your rental policies that are not included in the generic form.

When you purchased your property you may also have agreed to a set of neighborhood rules, otherwise known as covenants, conditions, and restrictions (often referred to as CCR's), which typically cover things like whether you can park vehicles on the street, whether you can put up signs in your yard, whether you can have loud parties, and so on. You need to attach these additional rules to your lease. You don't want your homeowners' association to start fining you for violations of the CCRs that you didn't tell your tenant about.

Over the years we've added a few lease clauses that aren't included in any of the standard lease forms we've seen. These are clauses we've developed based on our experience or the experience of other landlords, which you may wish to consider adding to your lease.

Lease violations

At some point a neighbor will complain about your tenant's dog barking all night. Or the tenant won't pay their water bill for three months. You will send them communications about this and most of the time the tenant will deal with the issue. However, sometimes these issues can drag on longer than they should. To give tenants an incentive to deal with these issues quickly, we have a lease clause that specifies that if a tenant violates any provision of their lease, we have the right to charge the tenant an hourly rate for our time spent dealing with the lease violation. We don't charge tenants for routine communications or first time reminders. But if an issue becomes chronic, we can use this clause to motivate compliance, "As this is your second reminder, please note that any future reminders will cost X dollars to pay for our time in dealing with this lease non-compliance".

Additional household members

Only people named on the lease application may live at the property. This means no one may sleep overnight at the property unless they have another address that they consider their residence of record. (In some states, if a new roommate moves in, even if you don't know about it and never added the roommate to the lease, you must evict the roommate to get rid of him or her. The classic problem happens when a boyfriend or girlfriend moves in, then the couple breaks up and the person to whom you rented moves out. Then you are stuck evicting someone you never actually rented to.)

Pets

There are a number of items you will want to include in your lease relative to pets:

- Be sure to document any pets you approved as part of the leasing process. Specify that any additional pets require your advance written approval.
- Require that any pets be kept, maintained, and licensed in accordance with the regulations of the Humane Society and applicable licensing authority.
- If a tenant's dog bites a neighbor's child, it's likely that the neighbor will include you in the lawsuit. So you will want the tenant to indemnify and hold you harmless from claims made against you for their pet's behavior. This means that the tenant has to pay your legal bill and any judgment issued in a lawsuit relative to their pet.
- You will want to have the right to periodically inspect for pet damage and require the tenant to immediately pay for the needed repairs to restore the property to its original condition. The security deposit cannot be used for these interim repairs as you never want to decrease the leverage you are holding for future damages.

Batteries

Your tenant needs to replace the batteries in the carbon monoxide and smoke detectors as needed.

Repairs

On occasion, a tenant may find minor repairs are needed, such as replacement of the furnace filter. If your tenant is handy and wants to do the work themselves, you should be willing to reimburse them for the supplies. This way you don't have to run over and fix every little thing. However, you need to require that a tenant ask permission from you first so that you don't end up with a huge bill for a new furnace that the tenant decided they needed when all that was really required was a new furnace filter.

Roommates

If you are renting to more than one party and all will be sharing the costs, be sure to make all parties liable for the full lease—meaning that if one roommate doesn't pay his or her half of the rent, you can go after any of the roommates for the remaining rent. The same is true of damages: if one roommate causes damage, all roommates should be liable. This is because you do not want to put yourself in the position of mediating disputes among roommates. For example, the roommates may have agreed that one of them will pay the rent and the other will pay all other expenses, such as utilities. In a dispute you don't want to have sort all that out. So tell the tenants up front that you will go after whoever has the money and that it's up to them to sort out any disputes among themselves.

Landscaping

No modifications to the landscaping, such as cutting of trees or removal of bushes, without prior landlord permission. We knew a landlord who had a tenant cut down thousands of dollars' worth of timber on his property because the tenant wanted a different view.

Heavy objects

Pianos, waterbeds, and other heavy objects should not be permitted without your written consent. The reason for this being that not all buildings are intended for such heavy objects and it's easy to cause damage while moving them in and out.

Insurance

Don't forget to add the requirement for your tenant to have renter's insurance.

7. Setting Up Your Website

Your website will be your single most useful advertising tool. Even if you've barely used a computer, setting up a website is super easy these days and can be done by anyone.

There are a number of websites that help you to design your website. We use **www.jigsy.com** because their interface is so simple to use. Jigsy also has a program that enables you to pay a designer to do your website for you if you get stuck, so help isn't far away. Another reputable option is **www.godaddy.com**.

You are welcome to use our website as a reference for how to design yours (**www.limerickproperties.com**). Here are the elements that are critical to include on your site:

- **Rental policies**. This helps you to keep the allure of being a "big" company and to chase away scammers. It also saves you time because it cuts down on the questions a renter will ask.
- **Application form**. Have a PDF document that potential renters can download and send back to you.
- **Application fees**. If you set up a PayPal account, you can easily add a button to your website that allows people to submit their application fees to you electronically. If you collect fees this way, unhappy applicants can't cancel the check, should you have to turn someone down.
- **Property information**. As with the pictures, the more property information you can provide, the more you will differentiate looky-loos from seriously interested parties. Include floor plans,

school district information, and a list of appliances along with the usual information about rental amount and so forth.

- **Pictures**. Have lots of good pictures of your property—inside and outside. This will greatly reduce the amount of time you spend showing the property to people who turn out not to be seriously interested.

We strongly recommend that the property address *not* be included anywhere on your website or in any other advertising tools. This prevents people from bothering your existing tenants or, if the property is unoccupied, it avoids advertising to strangers that a house is sitting empty, just waiting for a wild party. Only give out the property address to seriously interested parties who want to come and see the property, and only after they have given you their contact information. Instead, your website might include a map that shows the general neighborhood location but not the actual property address.

8. Figuring Out the Rental Price

You want to get the highest rent you can. Well, sort of. What you really want is the most cash in your pocket. This chapter covers how to maximize your profitability, which might mean a slightly lower rental rate than the place right next door.

Setting the Initial Rental Rate
You have to be sensitive to how long your property sits empty while you are trying to find a tenant. Trying to get the highest rental rate can work against you because that process may take longer.

Here is a simple illustration. Say you think the right rent for your property is $2,550 per month, and at that rate it takes you a month to find a qualified tenant. During the first year, you will have collected eleven months of rent, because the place sat empty for a month—a total of $28,050. If you cut the price by $50, to $2,500 per month, you are likely to rent it sooner. In our experience, being 1% to 2% per month lower than the market reduces a property's time on the market by an average of two weeks. So, during the first year you would collect eleven and a half months of rent at the lower price of $2,500—a total of $28,750. Despite the rental price being $50 per month lower, you can collect $700 more in rent during the first year because you rented it faster.

We are always surprised at how small adjustments can make a sudden difference in the number of interested renters calling. Lowering the price by as little as $50 per month has often made the difference between no phone calls and multiple calls per day from prospective renters. If you aren't getting enough interest in your property, you may be priced too high. With your first properties, you will want to experiment to find the right balance between lowering the price a small amount and finding renters quickly in your market.

Reevaluating Rental Rates Upon Renewal
We typically sign leases for twelve months. At the end of the lease term, we evaluate the market with the same scrutiny as when we purchase a new property, to determine the appropriate rental amount. Our goal is to keep our rental rates near the market rate. If you don't keep pace with the market you can unwittingly place your tenant in the position of being well under the market—and when it finally dawns on you that they aren't paying enough, you may have to increase the rent by an uncomfortably large amount to get them back to market rates. We have found it's much easier to negotiate small increases every year, if warranted to keep pace with market rates, than to impose a larger increase less frequently.

Your annual rate review, however, should be balanced with keeping your good, long-term tenants happily renting from you. In the above example, if a house renting for $2,500 per month goes empty because a tenant doesn't want to pay an increase, that means you will have to turn the place over and will not be collecting rent for some period of time. Even if this time is short—say, two weeks—that's $1,250 in lost rent between tenants. You could afford to allow a tenant to stay in the house at $100 per month below market and still break even, because you don't lose the rent between tenants.

Your goal is to keep your tenants as close to market rates as possible while not turning the place over.

Figuring Out Market Rent
Our approach to determining market rent is pretty simple and is largely based on a review of what other landlords are advertising similar places for. If you are in a major metropolitan market, you can do this on **www.craigslist.com**. You can also use sites such as **www.forrent.com** or whatever other advertisers are common in your area. Just go to your local supermarket and look at the free "For Rent" magazines out front. They all have an online website you can use for research. Typically, these websites allow you to narrow your search by square footage and location, which will help you to find the properties that most closely match yours.

Depending on how familiar you are with local properties, a Web search may be sufficient for you to determine the right rental amount. If you are uncertain, it can help to drive by some of the advertised properties and find those that most closely match yours.

Throw out any prices that seem either much higher or much lower than the median for similar properties. You are not looking to be the cheapest property on the market, you are just looking to be slightly below most properties that are the closest match to yours.

9. Finding Tenants

When we first started our business, the scariest thing for us was wondering whether we would actually find tenants. After ten years in a major metropolitan area, however, we have found that there are always renters. In bad economic times, people who get foreclosed on or who can't afford to buy a home still have to live somewhere, and in good economic times the market is filled with inbound transfers from other locations. The question is not whether these people are out there but how to find them. There may be cities where a mass exodus has hit and the number of renters drops significantly, but hopefully you haven't bought property in any of those places!

How and Where to Advertise

When we first started out we advertised everywhere we could think of. We ran newspaper ads, we posted flyers at grocery stores and libraries, we ran ads in the "For Rent" magazines. Today we don't bother with any of that. We advertise for free at **www.craigslist.com**. We don't do any paid online advertising or any newspaper ads. Craigslist gets us tons of prospective renters within hours of placing a new ad. The same might not be true everywhere in the country—you may want to experiment a bit with some of the other options, particularly if you live outside a major metropolitan area. However, we occasionally try paying for advertising in other media, just to see if anything has changed, and find ourselves regretting it. All of our renters end up coming from Craigslist.

Wherever you place it, your ad should be a shortened version of the property information you have on your website and should include a link to the details on your website. This maintains the impression that you are a professional property management organization, even if you just have a couple of houses you rent on the side.

We used to put For Rent signs in front of the properties we were trying to rent, thinking that this would help advertise and would help people find the property when they wanted to view it. In practice, it turned out we never rented due to one of these signs. Eventually, we stopped putting signs out because the risk of advertising "This house is empty; please come party here" to a passersby seemed higher than any benefit we ever gained from the signs.

How to Handle Prospective Tenant Calls

When a prospective tenant calls, you are George from Charming Properties, not the property owner. At some point this will result in someone asking you a question like, "Do you think the owners would take a renter with a credit score that is below your minimum?" to which you can say, "No, I've never seen them compromise on that unless you have a lot of cash you can pay in advance." This makes it awkward for the potential tenant to argue with you, because you are just doing what the owner tells you. This will feel weird at first. Get over it.

When a potential renter e-mails or calls, make sure they have looked at your website before you set up an appointment to show the property. Your time is valuable, and if they've looked at the pictures it increases the likelihood that your property is one they are seriously interested in.

How to Conduct a Showing

Whenever possible, group showings together in open house style, as in "We will be showing the property at 3 p.m. on Saturday." This has several advantages. First, you will spend less of your Saturday showing it to people at different times. Second, this is another way to send the message to potential renters that this is a real business. And finally, it tends to build a feeling among prospective tenants that they should hurry to get their application in before someone else snatches it up.

A word about security while showing. We have a rule that, because I am female, I can't do showings by myself at night, particularly to a single male client. We figure open house showings are safer because there are more people around. If a single male wants to see a property at a time when an open house is not available, then my husband does the showing or I take someone with me.

If you are showing a higher-end property, you may want to "stage" a property before showing it. You don't have to fill the place with furniture the way a real estate agent would to sell a high-end property. You just need a few nice touches here and there—some nice towels in the bathrooms, a few platters or dishes arranged artfully on the kitchen counter, that sort of thing. We do this with stuff from our own house, so it doesn't cost anything, but if you do purchase items for this purpose it will be a tax-deductible expense. Any time you can get a potential tenant to picture living in the space, it increases the property's appeal.

When potential renters show up, open the door and ask them to remove their shoes. This not only keeps the place cleaner but also sends the message that you care about the property and how it is treated.

Don't stand over visitors' shoulders the whole time they are looking around. Give them some space to explore at their own pace, but be easily available for questions.

Have some paper applications available to hand out, in addition to having the application available on your website.

10. Choosing a Tenant

You care about two things when choosing tenants: their ability to pay and whether they will take good care of the property while renting. That's all. You don't care if they are purple or come from Mars. You don't care about their sob story, no matter how sad. That isn't to say you should be rude and not listen patiently while they tell you their story, but on the inside you should be saying to yourself, "*Next!*". If your spouse is particularly bighearted and likely to get drawn into trying to "help," then don't send him or her to screen renters when you show the property.

This is the part where you learn to be a "big bad landlord." It's also the thing that makes the difference between renting to someone you have to pay thousands of dollars to evict or clean up after, and renting to someone who pays their bills and takes care of your property. If this part is hard for you, don't get into the rental property management business. One bad tenant selection can undo a year or more of profits.

Being clear that ability to pay and take care of the property are your *only* criteria for choosing a tenant also helps keep you clear of accusations of illegal discrimination.

Credit Checks
Virtually every horror story we've heard from other landlords starts off with "I should have run their credit but. . . ." Run credit checks, period—no exceptions. You will run the credit for all adults that will live at the property as well as any co-signers. We once had a renter falsify a social security number. She just kept "accidentally" dropping a digit. It turned out she was

a scammer who had no money and bad credit. We were all set to rent to her because in person she seemed like she was on the up-and-up. We thought something was wrong with the credit check system until we finally caught on. It was only the credit check hurdle that prevented a disaster.

Our minimum requirement is a credit score of 600—which is fairly high in the rental market. Depending on what type of property you are renting, you may have to adjust this. But pick a minimum score you are comfortable with and stick with it. The credit check company where you set up your credit check account will be able to tell you the nonpayment odds for a given score.

The only exception we make to the credit score of 600 is for cash. We've seen several renters who had bad credit but who had a ton of cash. In one case a renter had bad credit because his business had gone bankrupt, but he had a ton of cash from the sale of his home. In another case a renter had bad credit because of medical expenses from a spouse who had passed away, but she had a large life insurance payout. In both cases we collected a year's rent up front. You can't get shorted on rent if you've already collected it. Our only risk in these cases was what happened after the year was up—if the tenant had run out of money, we might have had to evict. But in both cases the tenant's financial situation had recovered after a year and the tenant was able to continue to pay rent for many additional years.

Income Ratio

Sometimes people will think that their budget can accommodate a higher level of rent than is truly sustainable. You need to verify whether a renter can afford the rent based on his or her current level of income. Look at how much income she has, how many debts or loans she has, and how much she has remaining for rent. This is the same type of criteria that banks use to determine whether someone can afford a loan.

In order to calculate the "ability to pay" ratio, we divide the rental amount by a renter's gross monthly income (income before taxes), and we won't rent if this ratio is higher than 30%. If there are roommates, we add the income of all the roommates together for this calculation. In the case of retired people we use the income from their investments (but not the investments themselves) plus the income from social security. Any form of income, such as child support or alimony, can be included in the calculation.

If the renter has unusually high amounts of debt or loan payments that show up on his or her credit report, then you need to apply some judgment in applying the 30% ratio, because that person may be overly burdened by debt.

Income Verification

Verify a renter's income as documented on the rental application. If they are employed, you will need to check with their employer. Most companies will require that you submit a signed copy of the application to ensure it's OK to release confidential salary information to you. It's not uncommon for people who have just been fired or laid off to try to move to a less expensive apartment before anyone figures out that they no longer have an income. So asking to see past pay stubs isn't a substitute for verifying current employment directly with the employer. If they are retired, ask to see a recent bank statement showing their retirement funds and a recent social security check.

Prior Landlord Reference

If possible, check with renter's previous landlord to find out whether they paid their rent on time and whether there was any damage when they moved out. Don't call their current landlord, because the current landlord might say anything to get rid of a bad renter. Ideally, you would call the previous landlord because he or she will have no incentive to withhold information about problems with the tenant.

Length of Stay

Given a choice, favor a renter who plans to stay indefinitely over one who is transient. As we've seen, turnover will greatly affect your profitability. Every time you have to find another tenant, there is a period of time when the property is empty and you aren't collecting rent. The longer a tenant stays, the more money you collect.

You also will want to look at when the renter wants to move in. Sometimes renters will look for places thirty days or more in advance of when they want to move in. If you have other qualified renters who want to move in right away, it may be more profitable to choose one who wants to move in sooner.

Cosigners

We have sometimes accepted cosigners, particularly when we have properties located near a college and parents are willing to cosign. Make the cosigners a full party to the lease, which means they are liable for the rent and damages just like the tenant. Run the cosigners through the same credit check/application process that you use for the tenants themselves.

Section 8 Housing

At some point you will be asked whether you will take a Section 8 renter. Section 8 is a set of U.S. federal government–assisted housing programs in which the tenant pays a portion of the rent and the government pays the remainder. Some local governments (such as a city or county) have made it illegal for a landlord to refuse a renter solely because the renter is on government assistance. However, this doesn't mean that you must take a Section 8 renter ahead of other, more qualified renters. Find out whether it is illegal in your area to refuse a renter solely on this basis, then decide how you want to respond when asked whether you will accept Section 8 applicants. We simply say that we evaluate each potential renter on a case-by-case basis.

How to Turn a Renter Down

If someone completes an application and you determine that you don't want to rent to him or her, you will need to notify the applicant of this. The applicant is likely to be unhappy about your decision, so you need to be very careful what you say. Being as vague as possible is best. It is difficult for someone to argue with "I'm sorry, but you didn't meet the company's qualifications," whereas "Your last landlord told me you did a bunch of damage" is likely to get an argument about how rotten the applicant's last landlord was. Turn applicants down by e-mail if possible, because it's easier to control the conversation that way. If an applicant wants to argue, you can just delete the e-mail without a reply—this is much harder to do in a phone conversation. This is a good situation in which to "hide" behind your company, saying, "I'm sorry, but that's just the corporate policy" as opposed to "I decided to turn you down."

A special word of caution about turning down roommates. You can't release any confidential information about one roommate to another roommate. Say a boyfriend and girlfriend apply to rent a place together and you find that the boyfriend's credit report shows unpaid court judgments against him from a prior rental property. You call the prior landlord and learn that the boyfriend and his buddies had a wild party and tore the place up and the landlord had to sue for damages. If the girlfriend calls you and wants to know why you turned them down, you cannot tell her what you learned about her boyfriend because that would be a violation of the laws protecting the confidentiality of credit information.

11. When Your Tenant Moves In

You've decided who you want to rent to and have agreed upon a price. You are almost ready to start collecting rent checks—but not quite.

Signing the Lease
Tell your tenant that you will continue to advertise the property and accept applications until you receive both the signed lease and a cashier's check for the damage deposit and first month's rent. You don't want to stop advertising, in case the tenant changes her mind a week from now, when she was supposed to move in. That's a week of lost rent, if you have to completely restart the process of advertising for a renter. So you want the tenant locked in. Insist on a cashier's check, because if the tenant gives you a bad check for that first month, you will find yourself completely unprotected against damages.

Setting Up Utilities
It will be up to your tenants to set up the utilities in their name. This is where having that move-in information sheet you developed earlier comes in handy. Some utilities require the landlord to call them first and let them know that a new tenant is moving into the property, before the tenant can call and give them payment information specifics. You will have to work with each utility in your area to determine what their process requires before a tenant moves in.

<u>The Walk-Through</u>

You and your new tenant will need to do a walk-through to review the status of the property before he moves in. During this walk-through you need to document in writing any existing damages—anything from scratches in the walls to a hole in the carpet. This is critical, because if you want to keep any of the tenant's damage deposit when he moves out, you must be able to prove that the damage did not already exist when he moved in.

During the walk-through, take the time to call attention to key lease clauses that you think people may not have noted. People often won't read all the fine print when they sign your lease. For example, if you are renting to a single person, you may want to call attention to the fact that they can't have their girlfriend or boyfriend move in without your permission. You also will want to call attention to the fact that the tenants need to get their renters insurance in place and have a copy sent to you.

If you have younger tenants, such as college students, remember that they've never had to take care of a house themselves and therefore may not know what maintenance issues to look for. For example, walk around the property and ask the tenants to inform you if the caulking around the sinks cracks or if moles start digging up the yard, so that you can attend to these things before major damage occurs. We've had good luck with setting expectations up front, before problems crop up.

12. What to Do if Someone Doesn't Pay

OK, so you've religiously done your credit and background checks, but despite all that due diligence your tenants miss a payment. Do not lend a sympathetic ear to their woes. Send them immediate notice that they are overdue and indicate what the late charges are. If they don't respond within a few days with payment of both the rent and the late charges, then you need to proceed as if you are going to evict them. It sounds cruel, but the reality is that in most states eviction can take weeks, if not months. Thus, every day that goes by might well be a day for which you never collect any rent. Your job now is to minimize that length of time—which means you start the proceedings ASAP.

Unless you are super experienced with your local eviction process (and hopefully you never will be!), this isn't something to attempt yourself. We do everything ourselves, but not evictions. We've never had to go beyond threatening an eviction, but nonetheless, we call an attorney when we get to this stage. Judges are notorious for being sympathetic to someone who is about to be without a place to live. One small paperwork mistake on your part during the eviction process may delay the eviction, and in the meantime you are still making your mortgage payments without rental income.

We once heard about an attorney who posted the legally required eviction warning notices telling tenants they had *seven* days to pay or they would be evicted. The law required *three* days. So even though the attorney gave the tenant more time to pay than was legally required, this paperwork mistake meant that the entire two-month eviction process had to be restarted. If an attorney can make this kind of mistake, it is a sure thing you will too, if you try to stumble your way through the process yourself. There are lots of attorneys who specialize in evictions and charge only a few hundred dollars to do it. Go find one locally and set them loose.

Once you start proceedings, one of two things will happen: either your tenants will find a way to pay the rent, in which case you can decide whether to continue with the eviction, based on your judgment about their future likelihood to pay, or you will have to evict them. In either case, there is no harm—and only upside—in beginning the eviction process quickly if a tenant misses a payment.

13. Concluding Thoughts

We hope this book has provided you with some useful advice. As we mentioned in the introduction, it isn't meant to be comprehensive, but is intended to at least introduce you to all the topics with which you need to become familiar if you are to be a successful landlord and property manager.

At this point, you will want to decide whether being a property manager is for you. You will want to consider whether you want to do all the things covered here, and also whether you have time to do so. We estimate that doing all the work described in this book averages about twenty hours per year per rental property. Some months all is quiet and there is nothing much to do, and then at other times we have several properties turning over so we are doing a lot of showings. Hence, some flexibility to deal with whatever comes up is a must.

If you have comments or questions about the content of this book, please don't hesitate to contact us. You can find more information about us and our consulting business, designed to help you get up and running smoothly, at **www.limerickproperties.com**.

ABOUT THE AUTHOR

Melissa and her husband have owned and managed rental properties for more than ten years. They have never been shorted a single penny in rent owed and have kept a 98% occupancy rate over the entire period. They now consult with first-time property managers, helping them to get their businesses started, offering practical advice and help every step of the way. Check out their website at **www.limerickproperties.com**.

www.ingramcontent.com/pod-product-compliance
Lightning Source LLC
Chambersburg PA
CBHW051255170526
45165CB00004B/1729